PEACE OF MIND

Peace of Mind

Published 2023 by Katharine Ryan Begley

Copyright © Katharine Ryan Begley
ISBN: 978-1-916544-10-9

All rights reserved. No part of this publication may be reproduced or transmitted in any form or by any means, electronic or mechanical, including photography, recording, or any information storage or retrieval system without permission in writing from Katharine Ryan Begley. The book is sold subject to the condition that it shall not, by way of trade or otherwise, be lent, copied, altered, resold or otherwise circulated without Katharine Ryan Begley's prior consent in any form of binding or cover other than that in which is published and without similar a condition, including this condition, being imposed on any subsequent publisher.

Publishing Information
Design & publishing services
provided by JM Agency

www.jm.agency
Kerry, Ireland

Peace of Mind

Poems of Praise

KATHARINE RYAN BEGLEY

*This book is supported by
Mary Ryan, also known as Nellie Kenny,
from Wexford town, Co. Wexford.*

Contents

Happy	8
Regrets	9
Today	10
I Know You	11
A Prayer	13
Gift	14
Two	15
One Day	16
Ireland	18
The Unknown Soldier	19
If	20
Mum	21
A Seed	22
Comfort	23
My Man	25
Times	26
Son	28
Mountains	29
Stroll	30
Words	31
Always	32
Faith	33
If I had	34
Brother	35
Travel	36

Look Back	39
Pray	41
Be Kind	42
Baby	43
Dwell	44
Mr. Thunder	45
Dog, Cat, Crow	46
Gossiper	48
Nan	49
No Matter	50
Steps	51
St Mother Teresa	53
Loneliness	54
Child	55
Dad	56
Knowing	57
Hope	59
Silence	60
Morning	61
Tomorrow	62
St John the Baptist	63
Hate	64
Perfection	65
Loss	66
Reach	68
Angel	69
God	70
About the Author	72

Happy?

Happiness I've heard it said is just,
a state of mind

Some people say search far and wide,
contentment you will find

It's also said take in your stride,
the troubles of the day

No problem lasts forever, no pain
is here to stay

For every sorrow in this world,
a blessings by its side

Every soul that leaves the earth,
replaced is a newborn child

For all the hearts filled with hate,
there's hearts abounding love

For every downpour in our lives,
a rainbow shines above

Each life on earth's a gift and
'all' are truly blessed

Peace with God is the only road
that leads to happiness.

Regrets

Regrets, if onlys will drain your life away,
ifs n' ands will torment the mind

The past cannot be changed!

Sun, rain, stars, shine on us,
sorrow pain and tears

Reminding us no matter what,
God's love protects us here

Memories are carried in our hearts
our minds and souls

We close our ears to the voice within,
that whispers *please let go!*

The feelings we go through make us
who we are

Connected nature's family,
our hearts as one entwined

Accept the cards life gives you,
time reveals its hand

All that's in the universe is
safe within God's hands.

Today

Today the world has changed,
all around is new

The sun now shines much brighter,
warmth's embracing you

Troubles in your heart will,
wither now away
Burdens that you carry,
have joined with yesterday

Sadness and despair belong,
now to the past

Hopes and dreams you long for,
reach out for you to grasp

Reflect a while, breathe in this
day, one moment at a time

When God made this morning's light
it's 'you' he had in mind!

I Know You

I know you, I've held your hand
each time that you've felt weak

My arms have gently held you close,
when words you could not speak

The tears you've cried I've counted,
each one I've wiped away

When you've been lost and lonely,
my light has shown the way

Through all your days I am with you,
from you I'll never part

I the Lord, I know you,
I dwell within your heart.

A Prayer

I said a prayer to God today,
and feel I don't know why

Words came out, tears welled up,
and I began to cry

I told myself it's stress in life,
the cause why I feel down

Or is it that I'm lonely now though
friends are all around

Then I understood my tears and
knew why I felt pain

With this truth an answer glowed,
my tears were tears of shame

The years had passed and getting on,
was foremost on my mind

Life's comforts I'd strived to get,
but God I left behind

So much time had passed me by,
since last I found I'd prayed

And only now I realised that,
by my side God stayed

My eyes were closed, I spoke the words,
my heart filled with love

I know the one that placed it there
was truly God above

Gift

A gift was given unto me,
so many years ago

It was said throughout my life,
this gift would start to grow

It wasn't very costly, though
priceless all the same

It wasn't something I could see,
nor did it have a name

I could not hold it in my hands,
to know that it was there

But knew it belonged to me,
when my lips spoke a prayer

Now that I am older, I understand it more,
the gift of love's been cradling me
since I was very small

Of all the treasures in my life,
the blessings I've received,

None can compare to the greatest gift
the day I first believed.

Two

God chose a man and a woman
not so long ago

In union, he blessed them
and watched their lives unfold
The love and faith within the man
steadfast he would be

The woman, kind and gentle she'd teach humility

Entwined as one, these qualities
Would stand the test of time
Life's shadows would be overcome
love and strength combined

Many years have passed since first
He made this match

Mum and dad, you're a living proof
God never makes mistakes!

One Day

One day I'll climb a mountain,
and rest upon the top

I'll ponder on the life I've led,
the life that I did not

I'll think of happiness I've known,
and also of the pain

I'll wonder what if time did turn,
how much of me I'd change

Mistakes I made, the falls I had
on those I would not dwell

Wisdom comes from yesterdays,
and I learned each time I fell

I'll think of all the universe,
and wonder then of God

Then understand He's walked with me
on every path I've trod

So when I'm on that mountain
reflecting on my worth

I'll realise how precious I've been
to Him since birth

I'll know He's reaching out to me
in everything I do

For in Jesus I've got heaven,
and the earth's my stepping stool.

Ireland

Ireland is a symphony of classics,
rolled in one

A poet's inspiration, declaring
true loves song

An artist's dream of beauty, such
splendour to behold

A writer's muse discovered,
unlocking thoughts of old

Majestic mountains, shores of gold,
rivers running wild

Fields aglow all around,
protecting nature's child

A piece of heaven placed on earth,
unchanged from cares of woe

Ireland is to all-refreshing,
to the Soul.

The Unknown Soldier

Whose is the grave that's marked unknown
in the land of soldiers passed on

Whose was the life that was lost in the fight
for the land that we now walk upon

Did anyone weep for this man with no name,
does anyone care how he died

Is anyone left who fought with him,
or do they all lay by his side

Was he a kind and gentle man that
put his life on the line

None will know what he was like
for not even his name can they find.

If

If I was good, I'd not
forget to pray
each night and day

If I was good
throughout my life
I'd never lose my way

I never would be tempted
to walk the darker road

I'd walk upon the steps of light,
the footprints of our Lord

I would not close my eyes and ears
to suit my worldly needs

I'd listen to love's whispers
gently guiding me

If I was good, I'd praise Him
with every word I spoke

Yet bad or good, eternally
my heart and soul He owns!

Mum

How lost I would have been
without you by my side

The paths I blindly wandered
when choices seemed so hard

My judgement tripped me many times
your arms would raise me up

The stumbling years revealing that
love's a constant touch

Your guidance was a haven, a place
to hide for me

The home in which throughout my life
your heart it held the key

My memories are paved with light,
because God made you mine

He placed a star within my life and
Mum, you make it shine!

A Seed

We're given each a seed of faith;
this seed you must nurture.
Guard it, water it, and it shall grow
and grow, until it becomes a mighty force
within you that's indestructible.

It is your only weapon of survival, and
it will serve you well, as you serve it.
Neglect your seed, and it will die and
buried with it shall be the truth.

The truth is the word of God.

Cherish the seed you have been given,
and all the days of your life,
it shall cherish you.

Comfort

Have comfort in the knowledge that
you are truly loved

That all the good things in your life
are given from above

If things go wrong, do not despair,
Nor think yourself alone
But listen, for within your heart
His love shall call you home

Don't look for signs in worldly things
in answer to a prayer

For God has written you a book,
all answers lie in there

If things don't go as you would wish,
don't look for who is liable

Read God's book, for all you need
He's written in the Bible.

My Man

My man John is really a pain
most of the time he's a non-stop complain

He moans about life and what he can't have
another woman, I'm sure, he'd drive mad!

We don't go to discos, he's not into them
we go to the pub and drink pints with his friends

He loves the Dubliners and most Irish bands
as he would say, 'their music is sound'

Now, my man John is far from romantic
mention a ring, and boy will he panic!
Talk about love, he'll have none of that,
before the words are out, his cases are packed!

I'm not after his mansion, his Porsche or his yacht,
or all of that money he hasn't got!!

Now, I'll tell you a secret, but don't breathe a word
I really do love him; yes, I know he's a nerd!

But if I could choose from all of the men,
my man John I'd never trade in!

Times

When times are hard, and fortune
never seems to go your way

And failure seems the only thing
you're seeing day-to-day

When giving up is easier than
trying once again

You'll need these words, for in them
is how you're going to win

Why embrace doom and gloom and
make yourself feel bad!?

When hope hugs back and gives you
that good feeling you once had

Forget mistakes, they're in the past
it's now when dreams come true

The world is holding out its arms
with lots to offer you

Today's the day when failure you'll
never see again
For if it knocks take this advice,
never let it in!!

Eventually it goes away, feeling
very glum

For that's the day it knows it's beat,
and you my friend have won!!

Son

This time of year brings magic thoughts,
as memories flow to mind

Of little hands unwrapping gifts, of eyes
so full of shine

Excitement on that little face would
set my heart aglow

A smile that beamed so brightly
on that first sign of snow!

Such happiness is mine each time
I see you as a boy

My precious son, each Christmas Day
my gift from you is joy!

Mountains

I took some time to take a walk
down by the mountainside

Then raised my head in wonder for
their beauty stood so wild

They looked at me and chuckled, how
small I did compare!

A passer-by with mouth agape
eyes burrowed I did stare

I asked 'how did you get so big
and where did you come from?'

But all I heard was angry winds,
their song quite clear be gone!

As I turned to take my road,
I paused and looked again

And understood the challenge
God's mountains are to men.

Stroll

Today I'm going for a stroll
down good old memory lane

I see a child so fortunate
playing little games

The sound of laughter's in my ears,
a face so full of gleam

The love around so special, it's
almost like a dream

Happiness - the only thing that this
small child has had

And that's because I clearly see
the World's Most Loving Dad.

Words

These words, I know, can't heal your heart,
nor take away your pain

They do not hold a magic cure for
happiness again

They're just my thoughts to say to you
that love and comfort's here

The sorrow that you are going through
I wish you did not bear

I ask that God reach out to you
and hold you through each day

To give His love and strength to you
all this is what I pray

Always

There'll never be one moment when
you are on your own

There is no trial that comes your way
that you must face alone

Have courage when the strength you need
you cannot seem to find

For all the strength and love you seek
is with you all the time

Hold up your head, be glad of heart,
know comfort all your days

Believe the words of truth He spoke,
'I am with you always!'

Faith

Please help me keep my faith Dear Lord,
for I feel its fading light

It grows so weak, I fear that soon
my soul shall lose its fight

The flame that burned so brightly, this
night is growing dim

The strength I knew is leaving me, and
I fear my doubts shall win

Yet I know and feel your presence Lord,
and I know that you're still here

I know you'll never let me go for
I've asked you in this prayer.

If I had

If I had words of wisdom,
I'd speak to ease your pain

If there was comfort in my arms,
I'd help you smile again

The sorrow that you're feeling now,
I wish you did not bear

I ask God's strength and love for you,
and know he'll hear my prayer.

Brother

The love I feel for you inside
can never be destroyed

For memories they planted it
when you were just a boy

No deed you do, no word you speak
can change what's in my heart

For every blessing shined on you,
I take a silent part

Although our roads are separate,
and words are not exchanged

My heart is where my brother,
though distant, still remains.

Travel

I travelled near, I travelled far
in search of the divine

The seas I sailed, the lands I roamed,
the mountains I did climb

I looked behind, I looked ahead, and
laid awake at night

I cried 'Dear Lord I've tried my best,
yet cannot see your light'

Then the softest voice I heard, and
this it said to me:

*'I am the light of all the world, look
harder and you'll see*

*Why have you searched in every place,
and travelled far and wide?*

*Do you not know, my loving child, that
I would never hide*

*I've held your hand, I've called your name,
and still you have not seen*

*My precious child, within your heart is
where I've always been!'*

Look Back

When you look back upon your life,
and think yourself as plain

I'd ask of you to concentrate and
take a look again

You'll see a girl who's good and kind,
and always tries her best

Whose thoughtfulness to others stood
out from all the rest

You'll see a beauty, true and fair
that all around you see

Of hearts been touched by honest love
that every person needs!

Look through my eyes then you'll see
clearly who you are

A precious gem that's searched for
by others near and far

A rarity that's priceless is what
I've always known

A wealth that others dream of,
to them has not been shown

And when it is you'll hear them say,
'There's someone I've just met

the dearest person in this world,
her name is Bernadette!'

Pray

If ever you have said a prayer
and wonder if God heard

If your wish went by unanswered
and you feel He spoke no word

Search your heart more deeply,
and try to understand

The wisest of the wise on earth
no concept of God's plan

We ask for graces from Him
some big and sometimes small

There's times we feel within the wind
our reverence words may fall

We're all not wise, we're all not rich
there's none of us the same

But one thing stands since time began
the only thing unchanged

And that is God, His love for us
His faith in every soul

He chose the time we should be born
He'll judge when we should go

And when He calls us back to Him
it's then we'll truly know

That God has always heard our prayers
sometimes the answer's 'No'.

Be Kind

One kind word is all it takes
to touch a lonely heart

A warm embrace and silently,
a burden's cut in half

One moment in a life that's shared
can fill an empty space

A simple smile that's offered
transforms another's face

An act of love, however small,
will touch a distant soul

One kind word will always make
someone's world feel whole!

Baby

God gave a special order
to angels at his side:

'A prayer, he said, I'm granting!
In heaven from a child!

Ingredients - the purest heart
to always show there's joy

Two stars be placed within the eyes
that light shall be adored

A mouth sculpt from a rainbow,
life's colours it will show

The final gift I breathe upon
My gift, a shining soul!'

Dwell

Don't dwell upon the path you've walked
no need to look behind

Today the future calls to you,
where happiness you'll find

Judge not yourself by others' eyes
that cannot really see

The eyes of God are in your soul
life's grace He gave to Thee

Discard all clouds and shadows
fear not the lonesome dark

God burns his torch of burning love
Forever in your heart!

Mr. Thunder

Poor old Mr. Thunder, alone up in the Sky
Crying oh, so many tears
and stopping just to sigh

Sniffle! Sniffle! Sob! Sob! It's all he seemed to do
until one night he jumped with fright
when a voice yelled 'who are you?'

'Oh, I'm just Mr. Thunder, and all I do is cry
You see, I have no friends at all (Sob! Sob!)
and really don't know why!?'

'I know why, dear Thunder - see, I'm alone like you
My laugh's so loud, my eyes so bright
but friends - there's none but you!

Please stay with me, dear Thunder, I'll look after you
The loudest people in the sky
such fun we'll have, us two!'

Thunder said, 'Oh gosh! Oh gosh! Just you and I together travelling?'
'That's right my friend, and by the way,
my name is Mr. Lightning'.

Dog, Cat, Crow

I saw a dog on his hind legs
 barking at a tree

And wondered what he fussed about,
 what was it he could see!?

Then I heard 'meow, meow'
 good gracious - it's a cat!

Half-way up the tree, he was
Now, what's he looking at!?

Then I heard 'squawk, squawk' on high right
at the very top

A crow was perched upon a branch
and 'squawk', he would not stop

The dog was barking at the cat
who really didn't care

For he was busy watching crow
who'd knew the cat was there

The dog, the cat, the crow - all three
I would not tell a lie

Stayed in that tree from dusk till dawn
'Till finally crow did fly!

Gossiper

Beware the one with ears pricked up,
for they'll hang on every word

Beware their warm and friendly smile
when they ask you 'have you heard?'

You'll answer no, then joyously
to you they'll spin their yarn

'It's terrible, a disgrace it is!'
now walks in the harm

Two more ears have heard their tale
now two more lips can speak

The gossip of the gossiper
is ready now to reap!

When they're asked 'who started this,
where did this rumour come?'

They'll point at you with that same smile
then will say, 'it's from yer one!'

And so beware the gossiper
for if they talk to you

Hold your tongue or the world will know;
then you will be the fool!

Nan

Whenever I've thought of you,
it always brings a smile

Of all the things I loved so much,
when I was just a child

Your handbag was a magic box,
which held goodies galore!

If mum said 'no' your loving voice
would say 'aah just one more!'

Bingo's a familiar word
that has your face attached

Bread and cheese, a sherry
enough to fill the gap

Kindness, love a cheeky smile,
a glint within your eyes

All these things come flooding back,
locked safe within my heart.

No Matter

No matter what your troubles are
no difference large or small

Each upset that may come your way
each time you slightly fall

The smallest fear you've ever had
is always known by God

Each step you've walked He's counted
on every road you've trod

So never feel that you're alone,
when shadows cloud your day

But speak His name and you will see
He's just a prayer away.

Steps

I want to get to Heaven,
but first I need a plan

What is it God will look for,
how will He know my name!?

Research is what I must do
to understand Him more

Before I stand outside His gates
I must know what's in store

Step one, introduction - I must
talk more to Him

He'll wonder who is knocking,
why should He let me in!?

Many of His children
He hears from every day

But me, I've been so busy
I just forgot to pray

My plan I'll mention, Jesus
our friend, His precious Son

I'll say He promised all who knocked
your doors remain open

Heaven's gates will open wide
And God will hold me close

Then whisper 'child, you're welcome home!
No longer are you lost!'

St Mother Teresa

I saw a little old woman
that heroes bowed before

I saw her capture millions
that looked at her in awe

Nations stood saluted
if the old girl passed their way

The hardest hearts would tremble
at words that she might say

Treasures gained throughout her life
were clothed upon her back

The ones she called her family,
diseased, the poor and sick

I wondered at the power
that came from one so small

How this one person changed the world
with love her only tool

Her life she lived so humbly
as a servant of the Lord

Yet in this frail old woman's hands
God placed a mighty sword!

Loneliness

When loneliness is
all around,
Know that I am here!

If sorrow seems
to fill your heart,
Know I'll wipe your tear!

When burdens are
too much to bear,
I'll carry them away!

If times are hard
and you feel lost,
I'll help you find the way!

When darkness seems
to cloud your dreams,
I'll hold you through the night!

For I, the Lord,
am by your side,
to darkness – I am LIGHT!

Child

A heart as pure
as Angels sighs
Two eyes that
see divine

Two ears that
hear the voice
of love
God's child till
end of time!

Dad

I've never really said the words
that in my heart I feel

How you have brought
my distant dreams so close
and made them real

Memories are cherished thoughts
to which you paved the way

My strength, it comes from your dear love
and every word you say

There's many blessings in my life
for all of these I'm glad

But what really makes me smile with pride
Is saying 'that's my dad!'.

Knowing

The qualities that shine from You
have lightened up my life

My problems that seemed heavy
you shared and made them light

All worries seem to fade away
whenever You're around

For if I fall I know it's You
who'll lift me from the ground

When times are hard, and I feel lost
I never now despair

The thing that gives me comfort
Is knowing You are there.

Hope

When sorrow seems
to fill your heart,
and all you feel is bad

I'm going to share
a truth with you,
about a friend I have

It happened on a lonely night
when all I thought was lost

Upon the wall a picture hung
of Christ upon his cross

I raised my head as tears ran down
and looked at him and said,

'With all my heart I ask of you
to take away my dread!'

With arms stretched out
I heard him say,
'Be still for all is well!
My love for you is mightier
than any pain you feel.'

My tears were dried,
my heart was light
Once more he softly spoke

'To others tell
when in despair
In Me, they shall have Hope!'

Silence

As Silence now surrounds me,
I reflect upon my years

The happiness, the joyful times,
sorrow, pain and tears

With Nature's beauty all around,
it's then my eyes can see

How much God's love is in this world,
How much He cares for me

And so when I feel down at heart
I say a silent prayer

His promised words echo back
'Know peace, for I am here!'

Morning

The mountain mist glides playfully
and rests upon the ground

Blindly sending echoed chills
to nature all around

The rising Sun will not play
so stirs the birds on high

Their morning cries awaken all
for slumbers been denied

The flowers force their heads erect
in search of warming light

Alerting bees who patiently
await the welcome sight

The day has dawned and swept away
what mischief left behind

Embracing life's true harmony
Until once more nighttime.

Tomorrow

Lord, please don't let mum see our tears,
nor see our broken hearts

Protect her from the pain we feel
now we've had to part

Lord, show her the abundant love
that's filling up this day

She built it with her gentle soul
In her precious, loving way

Please tell her Lord, 'be happy mum,
you're always by our side!'

Time cannot dim the love we share
for our hearts know you're alive

Rest now mum, when you wake up
Your loved ones will be there

We place you in the greatest hands
Back to God's loving care!

St John the Baptist

'Did you hear my voice?', I shouted loud
to all, 'He's on His way!'

The ground I paved before Him
less stoney ground was laid

I leapt for joy within the womb
When His presence touched my soul

Burning love embraced my heart
the Glory I made known

I told to all follow Him the place,
I could not go.
For I knew my task was over and
God would call me home.
My life was isolation living off the land,
a prophet wild with madness
for they would not understand.
They killed me lest you listened
to silence all my words.
My voice shouts loudest now to all,
'Jesus Christ is Lord'!

God's Word will not be quietened,
truth has been revealed!

Hate

She is black with an accent,
I hate her!

He is brown with a turban,
I hate him!

She has her head covered, a Muslim
I hate her!

He's an Asian, doesn't speak English,
I hate him!

She's wearing a sari,
I hate her!

He's a Jew on a cross,
I nailed him there!

My name is hate, follow me,
I'll lead you to *despair*!

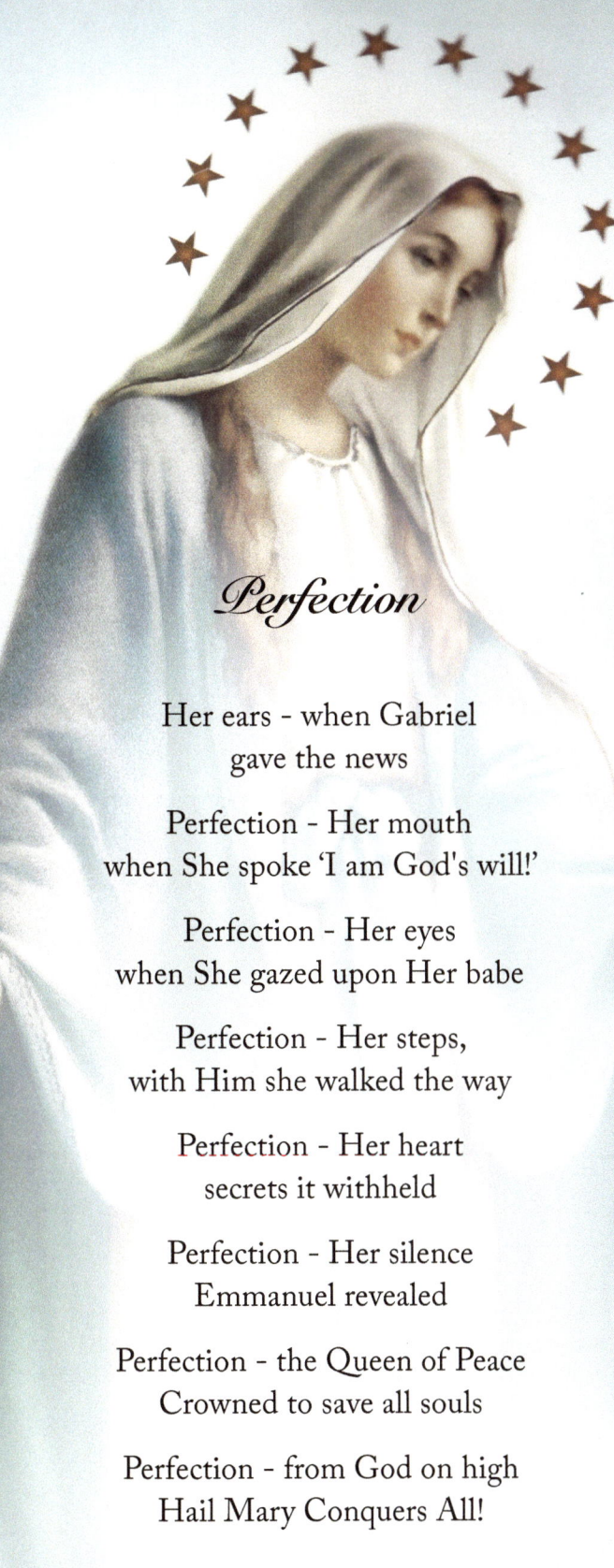

Perfection

Her ears - when Gabriel
gave the news

Perfection - Her mouth
when She spoke 'I am God's will!'

Perfection - Her eyes
when She gazed upon Her babe

Perfection - Her steps,
with Him she walked the way

Perfection - Her heart
secrets it withheld

Perfection - Her silence
Emmanuel revealed

Perfection - the Queen of Peace
Crowned to save all souls

Perfection - from God on high
Hail Mary Conquers All!

Loss

I know the pain you're in and the
reason you feel lost

I understand your heartache of
love and of the loss

The world is very different when
a part of you has moved on

The missing piece of who you are
now searches to belong

All the love's beside you still
It hasn't gone too far

The pause of life will play again
when you're ready to take part

It isn't far, clear your mind
push cloudy veils away

You will see eternally
Love is here to stay!

Take your time be comforted
in what will always be

The whispers are beside your ear
asking you to see!

Smile once more, soon you will know
love is never gone

It's walked into another room,
Love's found a brand new song!

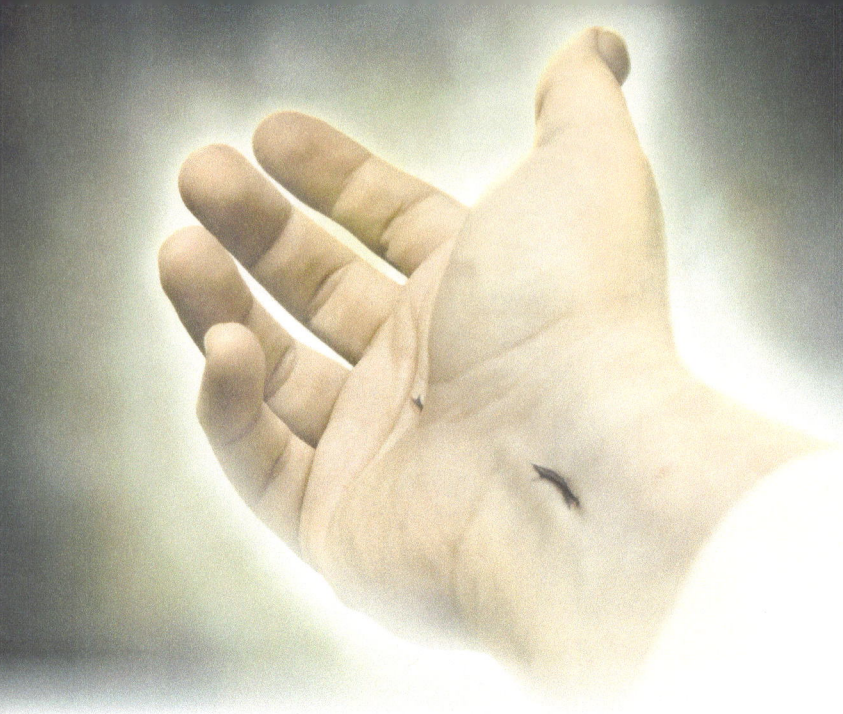

Reach

There is a hand reached out to you,
it's been there all the time

When tears and sadness overwhelm,
around your heart it binds

Life's paths are full of bumps and curves,
but solid ground you'll find

No one's heart is lost for long,
God's sheep are always found!

Love for you is reaching out,
still waiting for your grasp

Beside you, its forever stretched
'Reach back!' is all that God asks.

Angel

We were given an angel, Adelle was her name
whose true honest heart had no knowledge of pain

Her shining white soul outshone all the stars;
Her pure silent voice sang music afar!

God looked down from heaven,
He saw her and smiled,
then whispered so softly
'I love you my child'

He stretched out his arms and took her above,
Where our daughter Adelle shall know only love.

God

How much you are truly loved
no time can ever change

The messengers He sent to us
His prophets - all were slain!

His mercy is infinite
He'd send his only son

Surely he'd be listened to
Light from light is one!

Heaven's lamb was tortured
embracing death, his cross

In agony, mercy stretched
to all - His kingdom promised!

Repeating his message
'My father's love is here right now!

I am sent to change your hearts'

Echoing to all the world-
'My God. how great Thou art!'

About the Author

Born in London, Katharine Ryan Begley has lived in Co Kerry, Ireland, for the best part of twenty six years, with her husband John, the subject of the humorous poem 'My Man'. In addition to being a source of poetic inspiration, Katharine has had six children with John, Thomas, Adelle, Shauna, Connor, Molly, and Alice, all of whom she is very proud of.

While marked with a blessed modesty, Katharine's ability to convey deeply spiritual experiences in simple language is a gift. Her ethereal, deceptively plain verse is sure to delight both the spiritual and readers searching for something deeper in their lives. For Katharine, her poetry is a verbal hug, spreading radiant beams of comfort, hope and love to those that encounter it.

www.ingramcontent.com/pod-product-compliance
Lightning Source LLC
Chambersburg PA
CBHW040201100526
44591CB00001B/6